Quotable Animals

summersdale

QUOTABLE ANIMALS

Condition of Sale
This book is sold subject to the condition that it shall not, by way of trade or otherwise, be lent, re-sold, hired out or otherwise circulated in any form of binding or cover other than that in which it is published and without a similar condition including this condition being imposed on the subsequent publisher.

Summersdale Publishers Ltd
46 West Street
Chichester
West Sussex
PO19 1RP
UK

www.summersdale.com

Printed and bound by Tien Wah Press, Singapore

All images © Shutterstock

ISBN: 1-84024-598-0
ISBN 13: 978-1-84024-598-1

Quotable Animals

Animals are such **agreeable friends** – they ask no questions, they pass no criticisms.

George Eliot

Vanity is a vital aid to **nature**: completely and absolutely **necessary to** life.

Elizabeth Smart

There's no half-singing in the shower, you're either a **rock star** or an opera diva.

Josh Groban

Everything has two sides – the outside that is **ridiculous**, and the inside that is **solemn**.

Olive Schreiner

Peace is not a **season**,
it is a way of life.

Anonymous

Be ready when **opportunity** comes. **Luck** is the time when **preparation** and opportunity meet.

Roy D. Chapin Jr.

And God took a handful of **southernly wind**, blew his breath over it and created the **horse**.

Bedouin legend

The **cure** for boredom is curiosity. There is no cure for **curiosity**.

Dorothy Parker

Which of us has not been stunned by
the **beauty** of an animal's skin
or its **flexibility** in motion?

Marianne Moore

The **world** will never starve for want of **wonders**; but only for want of wonder.

Gilbert Keith Chesterton

The animals are much more **content** with mere **existence** than we are.

Arthur Schopenhauer

The **journey** of a thousand leagues begins with **a single step**.

Lao Tzu

I like **pigs**. Dogs look up to us. Cats look down on us. Pigs treat us as **equals**.

Winston Churchill

There is nothing **stronger** in the world than **gentleness.**

Han Suyin

Laziness is nothing more than the habit of **resting** before you get tired.

Jules Renard

To **wake** at the proper time; to take a bold stand and **fight**; to make a fair division (of property) among relations; and to **earn** one's own **bread** by personal exertion are the four excellent things to be learned from a cock.

Chanakya

An animal's **eyes** have the power to **speak** a great language.

Martin Buber

As **knowledge** increases, **wonder** deepens.

Charles Morgan

It **takes two** to get one
in **trouble**

Mae West

Whenever you **observe** an animal closely, you feel as if a human being sitting inside were **making fun** of you.

Elias Canetti

He who **sleeps** alone
stays long cold, two soon
warm each other.

German proverb

Correction does much, but
encouragement
does more.

Johann Wolfgang von Goethe

Mighty things
from small beginnings
grow.

John Dryden

He who would learn to **fly** one day must first learn to stand and **walk** and **run** and climb and **dance**; one cannot fly into flying.

Friedrich Nietzsche

Concentrate on finding your **goal**, then concentrate on **reaching** it.

Michael Friedsam

We are all **travellers in the wilderness** of the world, and the best that we can find in our travels is an **honest friend.**

Robert Louis Stevenson

Obstacles will look large or small to you according to whether you are **large** or small.

Orison Swett Marden

To acquire knowledge, one must **study**; but to **acquire wisdom**, one must **observe**.

Marilyn vos Savant

The **only thing** that should surprise us is that there are still some things that can **surprise** us.

Francois de La Rochefoucauld

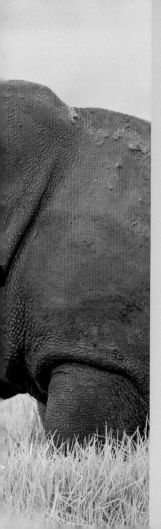

Happiness is like a **kiss**. You must **share** it to enjoy it.

Bernard Meltzer

When thou seest an **eagle**, thou seest a portion of **genius**; lift up thy head!

William Blake

The goal of life is **living in agreement** with nature.

Zeno

Every **animal** knows more than you do.

Native American proverb

The **family** is one of nature's masterpieces.

George Santayana

That which is called **firmness** in a king is called **obstinacy** in a donkey.

John Erskine

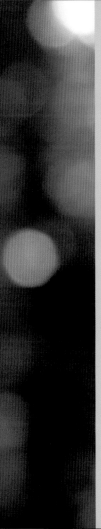

The key to **change**... is to let go of fear.

Rosanne Cash

Eternal **vigilance** is the price of liberty.

Thomas Jefferson

They that are on their **guard** and appear ready to receive their **adversaries**, are in much less danger of being attacked than the supine, secure and negligent.

Benjamin Franklin

Never follow the **crowd**.

Bernard M. Baruch

Life is nothing without

friendship.

Marcus T. Cicero

There is not one **blade of grass**, there is no **colour** in this world that is not intended to make us **rejoice**.

John Calvin

Do not **follow** where the path may lead. Go instead where there is no path and **leave a trail**. Only those who will risk going too far can possibly find out how far one can go.

T. S. Eliot

Patience is the companion of wisdom.

Saint Augustine

Solitude is as needful to the **imagination** as society is wholesome for the character.

James Russell Lowell

All of the animals excepting man know that the **principal business** of life is to **enjoy it**.

Samuel Butler

Quotable Dogs

£5.99

ISBN: 1-84024-537-9
ISBN: 978-1-84024-537-0

No matter how little money and how few possessions you own, having a dog makes you rich.

Louis Sabin

A stunning photographic book with quotes about canines, this delightful celebration of your best friend and loyal companion is a pooch of a gift for every dog-lover.

Quotable Cats

£5.99

ISBN: 1-84024-536-0
ISBN: 978-1-84024-536-3

Thousands of years ago, cats were worshipped as gods. Cats have never forgotten this.

Anonymous

A beautiful photographic book with quotes about cats, this delightful celebration of the world's favourite furry friend is the purrfect gift for every cat-lover.

www.summersdale.com